WISE
CHOICES

GW00786330

UNIV...... The real CHALLENGE

ANDREW KING

'Get wisdom, get understanding; do not forget my words
or swerve from them.
Do not forsake wisdom, and she will protect you; love her,
and she will watch over you.
Wisdom is supreme; therefore get wisdom.
Though it cost you all you have, get understanding.'

Proverbs 4:5-7

DayOne

Foreword

Last week a friend received a prospectus from a reputable university, which stated: 'This is a great place to study theology because it has great night clubs and bars.' My young friend from church felt utterly patronized and dropped the prospectus in the bin.

If that is the trendy way to sell student life, then this booklet is decidedly old-fashioned.

Andrew provides a survival guide for the serious Christian who wishes to put God first in all of life. He covers practical topics such as managing stress, time and money—as well as the more obviously Christian issues of unity, evangelism and church. Saturated in Scripture and years of godly reflection, Andrew provides invaluable and practical advice on applying our faith to all areas of life at university.

What is refreshing about this booklet is the blend of godly piety with smart pragmatism. If you want to make the most of being a Christian at university you will certainly drop the odd prospectus in the bin—but this booklet you must read, learn and inwardly digest.

Richard Cunningham
Director of Student Ministries
UCCF

The University: The real Challenge is not merely a survival guide for the potential overwhelmings of university life, but a timely and deeply biblical resource to help prospective students flourish in the academy, yet without being marginalized. As it turns out, university need not be a detriment to the Christian student's faith and devotion. In Andrew King's view, a little Scripture-grounded guidance and a regular dose of the Gospel transforms even the most hostile university campus into a sanctifying setting for believers.

John J. Bombaro, Ph.D. Director, The John Newton International Center for Christian Studies and Fellow, Dickinson College, Carlisle, Pennsylvania, USA

Christian students leaving home for university invariably find this experience their first and most challenging rite of passage. Andrew King's insights into university life from his own experience serve to make this book an indispensable tool to students and those who work with them.

Geoff Thomas, Pastor, Alfred Place Baptist Church, Aberystwyth, Wales

This short and easy-to-read book is filled with biblical common sense. Every Christian young person going to university will find it worth reading.

Stuart Olyott, Pastoral Director of the Evangelical Movement of Wales

Thoroughly biblical, short, easy-to-read and very well applied—I am delighted to commend this booklet! If only two of my school friends had read it before they went to university and shipwrecked their Christian lives. I really am going to give a copy of this to each of my godchildren.

Rico Tice, Associate Minister (Evangelism), All Souls Church, Langham Place, London

This booklet will help students greatly because it describes key biblical principles in a succinct manner.

Dr Stuart Burgess, Head of the Department of Mechanical Engineering, Bristol University

Alone in Cologne!

Be prepared

I was just five hours into a two-week tour of eight different countries around continental Europe. And for someone who had never been overseas, I was very excited! Going interrailing was certainly the thing to do. Lots of my friends had returned with great reports and fascinating stories. And at last my time had come. The only problem was that neither I, nor my friend, had thought to book our first night's accommodation. Before we set off our friends told us they had no trouble getting a bed each night as all the main cities had plenty of budget accommodation. We also knew that there were two youth hostels in Cologne and loads of cheap hotels so we were sure there was no need to worry about booking ahead.

We arrived in Cologne at 9pm (one-and-a-half hours late due to ferry problems) and the whole of Cologne was brimming with people and there was a lively atmosphere. However, we soon learnt that this wasn't the norm. A beer festival was going on. With all these extra people both the youth hostels were full. On top of this, the budget hotels and the more expensive hotels were full too! Even the sleeper trains were all booked as the remaining folk decided to move on to another place and travel overnight. A policeman then added to our woe when he told us that it was not safe to sleep outdoors as someone had been mugged recently when sleeping in a park.

Proverbs 14:15 says that *'a simple man believes anything, but a prudent man gives thought to his steps'*. Simply going with the flow and taking other people's words without you checking them is rarely wise. Circumstances change, assumptions differ and one person's idea of fun might be another person's nightmare!

Now my one-off accommodation problem was not such a tragedy, yet if you begin a major life episode like going to university without much thought, you may find yourself stressed and confused as you try and cope with the issues you will face and the decisions you will then need to make.

So, is university a good thing for young Christians? Is it a great maturing process, a time of spiritual growth and evangelism? Or is it a time of overwhelming worldly influence, compromise and drifting from God? Well, it should and can be the former: a good time to grow spiritually and to serve God well. But there are very real dangers to be avoided. I hope through this booklet to help you prepare to cope and where possible avoid these dangers. I want your days at university to be some of the best of your life. Why shouldn't you be used by God to do great things for him? Why shouldn't God use your witness to bring many other young people to faith?

What happened in Cologne? Well, on one last ditch walk around the centre my friend and I found a YMCA. Although they didn't have accommodation, a young man sitting there asked me whether I was a Christian. He had overheard my plea for a bed and, on hearing I was a Christian, he invited us to stay at his flat. Within half an hour we were at his flat eating a home-cooked hot meal and looking forward to a long, free sleep! Whilst God does certainly work in mysterious ways, on that night he taught me not to be like the simple man in the Proverb—just assuming all will be well. God doesn't want us to rely on his dramatic interventions; he wants us to learn and apply his Word. Don't start university like I started that holiday. I was so excited by other people's stories that I just assumed all would be fine. So remember Cologne—be prudent and think about what lies ahead for you, whether travelling or at university!

First things first

Repent and believe

When the apostle Paul wrote to the Corinthians he challenged them on the one crucial issue in life. He said *'Examine yourselves to see whether you are in the faith; test yourselves'* (2 Corinthians 13:5). Before we go any further, I would like to ask you whether you are a Christian. A Christian is an otherwise ordinary person who has experienced an extraordinary event: a new birth, the start of a spiritual life. And this spiritual birth will have involved a deep realization of your sin and hatred of it, and a turning to trust the promise Jesus Christ made that he saves all who believe in him. Whereas your ambition was once only to please yourself, now it is to please him. You love him, pray to him and willingly aim to obey his Word and serve him.

I'll just keep my nose clean then

If you have experienced that radical, life changing conversion, then praise God! You're a Christian and will be aiming to live a new life in service to God. If not, then I urge you to find out more about the Gospel—God's message of salvation—and pray to God to work in you and save you from your sins.

Being right with God—being a Christian—is the *fundamental* preparation for life. If you are not right with God, you are not prepared for general life, let alone university life. To prepare for university life without being saved is like going to fight in a battle without any armour or weapons; when it starts, you won't last a minute against the enemy. The Apostle Peter says in 1 Peter 5:8 *'Be self controlled and alert. Your enemy the devil prowls around like a roaring lion looking for someone to devour'*. What does he suggest we do to protect ourselves? He calls us to resist the devil. Paul tells us to put on Christian armour so that we can

> **'I thought that being a Christian was going to be church and avoiding the worst excesses of bad behaviour.'**
>
> *COLIN, NEWCASTLE UNIVERSITY*

withstand the devil's attacks (Ephesians 6:10-18). Yet this armour only fits Christians. It's not for those with just a passing interest or no time at the moment. If you're not a Christian then you are unprotected against the devil's schemes and therefore unprepared for life. So I urge you to repent, believe in the Lord Jesus Christ and you will be saved (Acts 16:31).

But if you are a Christian, then you will already be willingly submitting to Christ as your Lord—as your one and only boss. And one of the many parts of the armour you will use is the Sword of the Spirit, which is the Word of God. By obeying God's Word you will both show you are a Christian—and be protected from the devil's attacks.

To go, or not to go?

How to decide

C learly whether you should go to university or not depends on your own personal circumstances. But it is important that you think it through so you can make the wisest decision.

In the 1960s, around five per cent of school-leavers went to university in the UK. Since then, both the number of universities and the places they offer has dramatically increased. In 2002 around thirty-five per cent of school leavers experienced some form of Higher Education. And so, with many more places now on offer, it will be easier for you to get accepted on a university course somewhere. Many people today will tell you that you really do need to go because most jobs require 'graduate skills'. So don't be surprised if the teachers at your school or college urge you to go.

So what are the biblical principles you should apply in testing whether it is wise for you to go? Well, please consider the following three:

Contentment. God calls you to be content in whatever walk of life he gives you. The apostle Paul tells us *'godliness with contentment is great gain'* (see 1 Timothy 6:6).

Not everyone is suited for university. After all, it is intended to be a place of academic study and not everyone is cut out for that. Nor does everyone need to go to university. There are plenty of worthwhile jobs and careers that do not and will not require graduate skills. And so the first thing you need to do is to ask yourself whether you have the academic ability and the real need to go?

In the Bible we can see that God has saved people to serve him from a wide variety of backgrounds. The apostle Paul came from a more academic background and had been taught by Gamaliel who was a doctor of the Pharisees' law and one of the most revered teachers of his time (see Acts 5:34 and Acts 22:3). Today Paul would have probably gone to university and ended up with a Doctor of Divinity degree. We know God used him mightily in preaching the gospel, using his razor-sharp logic to confront the great philosophers of his time (see Acts 17:16-34). And yet in contrast to Paul, God also called the apostle Peter who came from a less rigorously academic background. Peter was a fisherman (see Matthew 4:18) and today he would probably have left school at sixteen and learnt his trade from others whilst earning a wage. God used him mightily in preaching the Gospel, particularly on the Day of Pentecost (see Acts 2:14) and also to go on to write warm pastoral letters to Christians facing hardship and persecution (see 1 and 2 Peter). So we can see from just these two examples that education was in no way a barrier to serving God. In fact God puts his people in all walks of life so that all sorts of people can be reached.

Unfortunately there has long been a view that the 'professions' are more important than the 'trades' with the idea that people with degrees are more valuable. But we have already seen that God certainly doesn't think like this. Peter was used to preach perhaps the most dramatic sermon of all time that launched the New Testament church! Perhaps the most compelling example is Jesus himself who chose a career as a carpenter before his ministry began (see Mark 6:3). There is absolutely nothing undignified or second-rate about a non-university career. Remember that pleasing God is far more important than keeping in with your school friends.

> **'I didn't have a clue about which course, if any, would have been right for me to study.'**
>
> NEIL, DATA AGGREGATION, N-POWER

Another great change over the last thirty years has been the opportunities for part-time university studies. No longer is the option between full time and not going. Many students have the opportunities to study while they work so they can both afford it and test out whether it is right for them. In addition, mature student opportunities are now available for those who didn't go to university when they left school, but wish to do so after a few years at work. These changes reduce the pressure of going immediately after leaving school. In a very real sense, opportunities now exist to go later on in life.

If academic study is something you don't enjoy or if the career you want to follow clearly does not need a degree, then think twice before deciding to go to university. God calls you to be content with the skills and interests he has given to you. Whether he is calling you to be a theologian, a fisherman or anything else, if you are a Christian you can be sure he has good works planned specifically for you (see Ephesians 2:10).

Realism. In deciding whether to go to university, you need to sit down and 'count the cost' both in time and money. Are you prepared to stick at your studies and keep going to the end?

You may well have the abilities needed for university and a degree may well help you in your career, but are you prepared to do what it takes for the next three to five years of your life? Some people start university in the autumn full of enthusiasm but soon begin to weary when the reality of hard work and long periods of study begin to bite! For some, the prospect of returning after the Christmas vacation is too much, and they drop out.

When Jesus was teaching his followers about the cost of being a disciple he taught an important principle. In Luke 14:25-34 Jesus confronted the issue of perseverance. He used a simple illustration. Suppose someone is about to build a tower. Well you'd expect that before launching straight into the action, he or she would first sit down and work out the cost and effort for the whole project. How long would it take? How many people would be needed to do the work? How much material, bricks and cement? What would be the estimated total cost? After considering all these things, the person would then decide whether or not to go ahead. Just imagine the embarrassment if he didn't count the cost at the start! The foundations are laid, the local newspaper has shown the artist's impression of the final tower, everyone is eagerly looking on … but the builder then announces that he has run out of money. He hasn't got enough to go further than the foundations! Why, people would laugh. They

> **'I knew what I wanted to do for a career so I didn't go to university because I didn't need to!'**
>
> *FIONA, NURSERY NURSE*

would certainly think the man foolish not to have planned ahead. And his chances of getting a job building another tower would be pretty low. No, we would rather expect the person to have sat down and thought it through. He or she would have saved up or secured a loan, employed the right people and planned out a work schedule to get the tower fully built.

Now Jesus used this illustration to show that Christians need to count the cost of following him. But the principle is a wider one that we can apply here. Before deciding to go to university, you need to count the full cost of what lies ahead. What do I mean? Well here are two things to consider:

a. Hard work. This is what university is about. A degree worth having will require you to attend your lectures and practicals, and to put in at least three evenings a week of intense study (I'm assuming a full-time course). The work you will do is designed to be hard, yet if you get accepted on the course that means you have proved you are capable of doing the work. You will have to re-read your notes and read extra material in the library. Are you prepared to do this for each of the years you are at university?

Now, I don't write this to make university seem unbearable! It is true that 'all work and no play makes Jack a dull boy'. But Jack is meant to be working a lot of the time. Hopefully the subjects you take will interest you in such a way that you will enjoy your time learning and researching. But do count the cost of evenings alone in private study, the discipline of attending lectures and handing work in on time. The students who get to the end and pass are the ones who counted the cost at the start and said 'Yes, I'm prepared to put in the effort, all of the time'. And in case you're feeling discouraged, the clear majority of students do pass!

b. Less money. Unless you're particularly 'well heeled', your years at university will not give you much extra cash. Sadly the days of student grants and bursaries are gone for the majority and so it's more likely that you will live on a low income, and probably supplement this with a loan or part-time job. On the other hand, your friends who choose not to go to university will be proudly spending their

first wage and, possibly, buying their first car! Are you prepared to wait a few years before earning a good wage? Do you see your university years as an investment for the future in such a way that you are willing, and content, to wait?

Whatever the rights and wrongs of student finance, the reality is that student life requires very tight financial management. This is a topic we will come back to later on. But the question here is whether you are prepared to accept this situation. Depending on your location and the type of accommodation you get, your 'spending money' might be very tight, and this will be for a number of years. Of course, the career opportunities and then satisfaction from study can more than make up for this temporary hardship. Most graduates do go on to earn far more over their careers to compensate for the few years of hardship. But do be sure that you are willing to put up with it at the time!

Honour. The third principle to be considered is that we should only do things that bring honour to God. Is the subject you are thinking of studying one that is suitable for a Christian? Now we must tread carefully here because depending on our starting point, we can reach different conclusions.

The apostle Paul is very clear in teaching us that *'whatever you do, do it all for the glory of God'* (see 1 Corinthians 10:31). This demolishes the popular idea that we have two lives: a spiritual one for God and a secular one where we can more or less live like everyone else. This idea was developed around the time of the so-called Enlightenment. Yet whilst it was correct in separating church and state, it is wrongly applied to suggest 'Bible-free zones' in our individual lives. Everything we do either honours or dishonours God. Whether it is singing hymns in church or watching television at home, each of these can bring honour or dishonour.

What is not so clear however, is how this is to be applied in each particular circumstance. I freely accept this is a difficult area. If we are to be holy and free from sin then perhaps we ought only to be taught everything from a biblical point of view? Yet, if such people or universities don't exist to teach us, perhaps we do need to study non-biblical perspectives as well so we can learn how to demolish false ideas and develop biblical alternatives? Or maybe we should be prepared to have an element of man-centred teaching if it nevertheless gives us a good opportunity to witness to unbelievers? I am not going to attempt to divide university courses into 'good' and 'bad'. But I do encourage you to look through the course aims and syllabus together with the reading and/or video material you will be expected to see. As this may seem daunting, this is an area where parents can help. Possibly the most efficient way to do this is to find a Christian who does know the subject so that he or she can point out the possible problem areas. Some university courses may actively allow a diversity of views as long as they are based on sound academic enquiry. Others may have a more fixed agenda to promote a particular (and usually non-biblical) set of ideas.

Don't be overwhelmed by the prospect of discerning what is wise to study. Our Heavenly Father knows we need help. In the book of James 1:5 we read *'If any of you lacks wisdom, he should ask God, who gives generously to all without finding fault, and it will be given to him.'* So, pray to God for wisdom, and do your homework to find out what the courses involve. We have the wonderful promise that God will give us wisdom to make a good decision.

So, to go or not to go? Being a university lecturer myself you may see me as somewhat biased! My university undergraduate and postgraduate student experiences were excellent. Now as a lecturer, each year I see undergraduate students developing personally, making lifelong friends and being stimulated by learning fascinating things from their subject. If you want to go for good reasons and have realistically counted the cost, then university can be a stimulating and rewarding place for you, too. But don't feel an unstoppable pressure to go just because everyone else is going. There can still be a wonderful life for you without a university degree!

That it may go well with you
Remember what your parents told you!

If you do go to university it's likely it will be your first time away from home. Sure, you may have had a few nights staying at a friend's house and a week or so on a supervised camp or beach mission, but going to university will be your first time *living* away from home. When you arrive at university you will meet hundreds of other young people all in the same boat. You will all be away from your parents and other figures of authority. What are you to make of it? Well, sadly the majority view that is likely to form in other students will be that 'this means freedom and at last you can do what YOU want! Get rid of all the boring, restrictive stuff your parents told you: now go wild!'

Our modern culture talks up the importance of individual freedom and champions the idea that we are free to do as we please. And so one clear temptation to you as a young Christian student is the notion that 'you are now a free agent'! Of course it may well be tempered with the recognition that your parents were trying to help. It is just that they set the boundaries far too close and don't appreciate that things are different nowadays.

But God doesn't want you to take that view. Far from giving you parents to cause you trouble, he has provided parents and local church leaders to care for you and, through an element of ongoing accountability, to guard you from danger. Our modern culture will tell you that parents' and church's views are old and outdated. But the Bible teaches us that parents have been given to guide, protect and equip us for a life that pleases God. Instead of throwing it all away, thank God for all this instruction and hold on to it. This is what God says to us in Proverbs 6:20-22: *'My son, keep your father's commands and do not forsake your mother's teaching. Bind them upon your heart forever; fasten them around your neck. When you walk, they will guide you; when you sleep, they will watch over you; when you awake, they will speak to you'.*

> **'There is pressure to conform and engage in sinful, unhelpful activities—especially in the first year.'**
>
> *JACOB, DURHAM UNIVERSITY*

Hopefully over the years your parents will have taught you from God's Word. If you are wise, you will remember and keep this teaching. Maybe you think this is open to abuse? What if your parents haven't taught you from God's Word but more from their own church tradition or personal preferences? Well, notice the caveat that God has wisely given in Ephesians 6:1, where he says: *'Children, obey your parents in the Lord for this is right. "Honour your father and mother"—which is the first commandment with a promise—"that it may go well with you and that you may enjoy long life on the earth"'.* Sadly some parents do read in far more than the Bible teaches. As a young adult away from home you are fully entitled to—and should want—a biblical explanation for the instructions your parents give. You are to obey them 'in the Lord', that is, according to the Bible. If they cannot give you a biblical reason then you are not bound by such over-demanding views. God has also wisely given us freedom of conscience on finer matters of detail (see 1 Corinthians 10:23-33) to guard further against any abuses of parental or church authority.

But the main point here is that you are still to keep hold of your parents' and church's teaching because God wants you to. This has no 'best-before' date on it. Rather it is there to guard and guide you through the rest of your life! Now that is radical—to show you love the Lord by keeping your father's commands! That is the witness your unbelieving friends desperately need to see. So how do we apply this? Well I have applications both for students and for parents.

A word to students

As a student be aware that you will most likely be living amongst other students who actively want to rebel against their parents' ethical and moral teaching. Don't be surprised or judgemental—that is just how you were before you received God's grace. Some of your friends may tell you you're only a product of your parents' indoctrination and what you really need to do is to show your independence by being different. But you should remember your conversion—it was real—it was personal. Remember that you are a Christian because of *your* faith not your parents' faith. It's not that your parents believe for you, it's rather that *you* believe the same truth they do. Are your friends unbelievers merely because their parents are too?

Remember also that you have been taught by God to keep your father's commands and not to forsake your mother's teaching. As a Christian, see all this as service for the Lord. He has asked you to do this, not merely your parents. Do this out of love to him and to bring glory to his name.

A word to parents

As parents, we can help our children in this matter by ensuring we bring up our children according to *biblical principles*. If God expects our children to keep our commands, we must be careful to teach them correctly *and to show them* that the teaching has come from the Bible. We should never merely say 'do this or that because I say so' but rather show them 'God says do this or that from this passage or that passage of the Bible'. In this sense, we start preparing our children for university from their early years by showing them we have a high regard for God's Word. If we don't, then we are leaving them unprepared. This is certainly a difficult task and we often fail—yet when we do, we must repent and return to our duty as parents. In 1 John 1:9 we read that '*if we confess our sins then he [Christ] will forgive us and cleanse us from all unrighteousness'*.

But also, and particularly as fathers, we must not exasperate our children in such a way that we tempt them to rebel. We've seen the teaching in Ephesians for our children, but God also teaches fathers in chapter 6:4 '*do not exasperate your children; instead, bring them up in the training and instruction of the Lord'*. Being negative, over academically demanding, or overly controlling can slowly 'wind up' our children so that they quickly uncoil at the first opportunity of freedom. As they grow up we need to balance our dreams for our children with their abilities. We need to counter our nervousness over their getting things wrong with their need to develop their own responsibilities. In short, we should increasingly treat them as young adults and order our home to give them fair rules and increasing responsibility for themselves.

As parents we should not succumb to our society's idea that parenting is really no more than just 'enduring the children until the first opportunity of getting rid of them'. Of course it's subtle. It's expressed by phrases such as 'Well, when you leave home you can do what you want, but while you're under my roof …' But how does that fit with Proverbs 6:20-22? Is our teaching just for while they are under our roof? We need to show our children a clear distinction between house rules and biblical teaching. The time by which we expect them to be home is a house rule that we set while they are living at home. When they are at university they will be free to set their own time. However, the teaching not to spend the evening in the *seat of the scornful* is a biblical principle that *applies at all times* (see the whole of Psalm 1). We therefore need to be careful to show our children that biblical teaching is not only for when they are at home.

And finally...

I don't suppose growing up will ever be easy. But the young Christian has a good foundation to build upon. University does and should involve a lot of change, growing up and independence. Yet we should never throw the baby out with the bath water by forgetting our parents' commands.

The Bathtub Curve
Dealing with stress

You can get a rough picture of what your stress levels are likely to be like during a University year by plotting stress on the vertical axis of a graph and time on the horizontal axis. Starting with the beginning of term in October and the end of term in June, the plot would look something like a bathtub shape in profile—high at the start (being a fresher and new to it all) but quickly settling down by mid November, then a fairly level amount of stress only to rise again at the end with summer exams!

It starts off with stress! Aside from all the frantic packing, the journey, the delays and the first sight of the tiny room that's to be your home for the next nine months, you have to contend with freshers' week!

Most universities have something called 'freshers' week' in the first week of term. It's a non-teaching week designed to help you (the fresher) settle in. During freshers' week you will be expected to digest a near impossible amount of information. You will get introductions to your accommodation, and the mandatory list of do's and don'ts. Then there will be tours of university buildings and facilities like the library, health centre and student union. You'll meet the main staff associated with your degree programme and have some introductory lectures and seminars to break the ice with your student group. If by the end of all this you can remember which building you are in and find your way back to your hall, then you will have achieved something! Everyone knows there is an awful lot to take in; but it is important for you to attend this so you can start the first week of teaching knowing what to do.

> **'Making Christian friends in my first week of university was a real blessing.'**
>
> *DELYTH, UNIVERSITY OF WALES, ABERYSTWYTH*

But aside from the business side of freshers' week, there will also be plenty of time and opportunities to socialize: most universities will hype up these events to excite you, and attract students to study in their particular town or city. The night life, clubs and bars will be well advertised and you'll receive a number of discount offers and persuasions not to be the odd one out who stays behind in your room. And after the night out comes the customary kebab, followed by a trip to the off licence and then on to the party at so-and-so's flat. And, temptation being what it is, the offer to stay the night with someone becomes far harder to turn down.

Toward the end of the week there is usually something called a 'freshers' fair'. This is usually laid on by the students' union (a student organisation run by students for students) and is where you get to meet all the clubs and societies under one roof. Each student club or society (together with a long list of

commercial banks and travel agencies etc.) will have a stall laid out in a big hall to 'sell their wares'. You will be cajoled into 'signing up' and parting with your money. Whilst there are plenty of free offers and the party atmosphere can be great fun, you can still face pressure—particularly from the new friends you go with—to join up to just about everything under the sun.

So how are you to survive freshers' week? Well, although it was written many years before the freshers' phenomenon, God's Word is again full of helpful yet uncompromising advice for you to follow. Jesus said in Matthew 5:14-16: *'You are the light of the world. A city on a hill cannot be hidden. Neither do people light a lamp and put it under a bowl. Instead they put it on its stand, and it gives light to everyone in the house. In the same way, let your light shine before men, that they may see your good deeds and praise your Father in heaven'*. What Jesus is saying is that you, as one of his disciples, cannot simply 'switch off' your Christian identity when the pressure is too high. In fact, the very essence of your identity is that you *show light at all times*. In Psalm One we are given a clear contrast between two ways of life: the godly and the ungodly. And part of this description shows that the godly Christian is happy (blessed) when he or she *'does not walk in the counsel of the wicked or stand in the way of sinners or sit in the seat of mockers'* (Psalm 1.1).

> **'I let everyone know I was a Christian and this forced me to stand up for what I believed.'**
>
> TIM, UNIVERSITY OF WALES, BANGOR

When Paul was teaching Christians living in Ephesus, he urged them not to *'grieve the Holy Spirit'* (Ephesians 4:30) and went on to warn them *'among you there must not be even a hint of sexual immorality, or of any kind of impurity, or of greed, because these are improper for God's holy people. Nor should there be obscenity, foolish talk or coarse joking, which are out of place, but rather thanksgiving'* (Ephesians 5:3-4). During freshers' week this kind of behaviour may be all around you, yet you are called to keep well away from this and rather to be imitators of God.

And yet our Heavenly Father is not unrealistic. He knows us intimately and knows that we are social creatures. The idea of 'shutting ourselves off in our rooms' should seem odd because it is! We have been created by God to be social people, to want to make friends and enjoy their company. And so the answer to this problem lies in the type of friends we make. We need to make godly friends. So, what application can we take on the matter of how to make good friends? Well, I have application for students, parents and church members.

A word to students

If you're a student don't hide the fact that you're a Christian. When I started as an undergraduate I wasn't a Christian, but when I went to another University as a postgraduate, I vividly remember the stress of first introductions with all the invitations I had to go to the bar. 'Maybe,' I thought, 'I should just go for a little while to get to know them? I might be able to witness to them!' In the end I didn't go and, on reflection, consider this was best. The likelihood of conversation leading to serious discussion on spiritual things was almost nil. And the environment was more likely to encourage me to fall into foolish talk and coarse joking. I still made good friends though, who respected my lifestyle and occasionally did discuss spiritual things.

Never let the aim of making friends lead to a compromise with ungodliness. Paul reminds us in Titus 2:3 that the grace of God teaches us that, *'denying ungodliness and worldly lusts, we should live soberly, righteously, and godly in the present age'.* Now of course this doesn't mean you should have only Christian friends or that you need to launch into a five-point sermon with each of your non-Christian friends! But it does mean you need to 'be open' about being a Christian. If you're not, you will not only be stressed by the situations that confront you, you will spoil your witness and dishonour God.

A word to parents

And parents, how can you help? Well, as your son or daughter will no doubt be concentrating on which course to apply for, you can help by ensuring there is a suitable local church nearby. What your son or daughter needs most is to find Christian friends and fellowship so they can enjoy a good social life without the pressures *always* to join in with non-Christians.

The early Christians described in Acts 2:42 *'continued steadfastly in the apostles' doctrine and fellowship, in the breaking of bread and in prayers'*. Each of these aspects of church life needs to continue with students, but the need for good Christian fellowship is particularly important for students away from home. In fact, I would go as far as to say that you're better encouraging them to go to their second choice university if their first choice gives no chance for them to attend a good church. The writer to the Hebrews reminds us that Christians should *'not give up meeting together, as some are in the habit of doing, but let us encourage one another, and all the more as you see the Day approaching.'* (Hebrews 10:25).

A few years ago a friend planning to go away and study explained she was deciding between two universities. She asked for some advice so I looked up the local churches and suggested she went to her second choice. Her first choice university was in a rural setting and the closest evangelical church was a twenty-mile car journey. Whilst it had a perfectly good course, she wouldn't be able to attend a church there because there was no public transport to it and she had no car. However, she went to her first choice. A few months later we learnt she wasn't attending that church or any other. So it didn't surprise us that when Christmas came she didn't come back to her home church. The temptations of worldly friends were too great and without the practical means, soon church attendance and Christian living became things of the past.

Of course that's just one case. But the important practical point for us as parents is to help our children find a church for when they are away. Obviously they need to go to a church that is 'biblical' and evangelical. It is more important to make sure it is within practical reach of their accommodation and will welcome them than to be of exactly the same 'grouping' as the church at home.

A word to churches

As church members what can we do to help? I have three suggestions.

If we have students from our church going off to university, we can keep in touch with them. The apostle Paul describes each local church as a body (see 1 Corinthians 12:14-27). In verse 21 Paul explains that just as the eye cannot do without the hand, neither can *at home* members do without *at university* members. In a very real sense, part of the body is away and should be missed. Depending on how well you know them (or how appropriate it is if you are single), you can help to encourage them both in their studies and their witness by writing the occasional letter or e-mail. Knowing that people back at home are interested and praying can be a great encouragement. It can also help news to flow back and forth so they still feel part of their home church.

You could appoint someone to be the main link member in your church to keep in touch with students while they are away. Each week or fortnight they would be able to feed news to the fellowship for prayer and praise. I heard of an excellent idea at one church where students back on vacation are invited (if they want!) to give a short report to their home church. They need

> A more radical way we can help students is to consider being their landlord or landlady!

only to speak for a couple of minutes to say what they have been doing and how they have been able to serve God in their new setting.

If, on the other hand, we have students joining us from a local university, we can consider a scheme to welcome and look after them on Sundays. Of course, this will depend both on the location and available helpers. But in the least we can make sure the university's Christian Union and Chaplaincy websites have our contact details.

A more radical way we can help students is to consider being their landlord or landlady! Most students have the opportunity to live in university run accommodation during their first year. This is usually worth taking both because it is cheaper and more convenient. However, for the remaining years, it is common practice for students to get into groups of four or five and then rent a 'student house' from a local landlord.

Although it ought to be straightforward to get a group of Christians together, this is not always possible. A Christian living with non-Christians can work well in some circumstances. Yet equally, it can be a very stressful and compromising situation when student parties, sleepovers and general social differences need to be negotiated.

As few of us would want to live with our own next door neighbours (although we would like to witness to them from time to time), we should see the difficulty for students. One Christian friend of mine singled this out as *the* most stressful aspect of her university experience. So why not consider adopting a second or third year student for nine months? If you are older you may have a spare room if your children have left home and got married. Some of you mums may enjoy doing some more mothering whilst some of us dads may enjoy some more income! Of course circumstances may not suit, but maybe you should give it some thought? My parents were so thankful for Christian folk who gave me accommodation whilst I was a student that they decided to take in someone for a short while when I had left home.

And finally…

Peer pressure and the stress of making good friends is a big issue. The best solutions are to be up front and honest about your Christian faith but also to find a good church where you can make Christian friends.

> **'The church was fantastic; an oasis in the chaos of student culture.'**
>
> *RACHEL, UNIVERSITY OF NOTTINGHAM*

The sands of time

Get your priorities right

In the previous chapter, I said that the stress curve most students experience was like a bathtub in profile: high at the start of term but also high at the end. This is because the summer is when most exams and project deadlines come. Yet a good deal of this work stress can be reduced through good time management. Poor time management throughout the year leads to high stress at the end. Often there is a direct correlation between time management and stress. And the easy tests for time management are lecture/tutorial attendance and meeting coursework deadlines!

I once asked one of my students who was hopelessly disorganizea ι. managed to pass his A-levels. His secret ingredient had been his mum! Sι. reminded him what homework he had, packed his bag each day, and even tolu him which classes he had! However, it's highly unlikely you'll have your mum with you at university to organise your time. In fact, I'm sure the thought of your mum walking around with you is most disturbing! So, on top of all your study time, *you* will need to manage your social time (which really means limiting your social time to allow for study time) and your day-to-day cleaning and possibly cooking time. Most importantly, you will need to organize your daily devotional time and church time.

Whilst this may all seem very obvious, almost all of my students accept this aspect of university life is far from easy when two or more things are competing for the same time slot. A common short-term solution is to stay up later in the evening to fit everything in. However, not many students can survive long with continuous late nights, insufficient sleep and irregular study patterns.

So what are the biblical principles when it comes to time management? The writer in Proverbs 6:6 calls us to take a look at the life of the average ant. *'Go to the ant, you sluggard; consider its ways and be wise! It has no commander, no overseer or ruler, yet it stores its provisions in summer and gathers its food at harvest. How long will you lie there, you sluggard? When will you get up from your sleep?'* We can learn at least three things from this passage:

Responsibility. As a young adult you are responsible for your own time management. Just as the ant has no boss to give time sheets or to direct its every move, so you will be increasingly left to plan and manage your own life. One of the most visible changes from school/college to university is the change from daily registration and break-time bells. At university you are free to come and go as you please. Now of course, just as the ant cannot choose when harvest time is, nor can you choose the time and place of your lectures. Yet the responsibility for you to plan ahead and turn up is entirely down to you. By the time someone has noticed you are absent, a couple of weeks may have passed, and that lost time will be very hard to catch up.

Planning. We can learn from the ant by noticing how it anticipates future demand for food and plans ahead. The ant gets the food for winter ready long before winter comes. And you need to be the same with your studies so that work starts well before the deadline to submit the work. The example of the ant is staggering because it doesn't have anyone to remind it, yet gets everything done on time! When it comes to a coursework deadline, you should always assume something unexpected will happen the night before. Assume the book will not be in the library the day before and assume the printer will not be working! At best you can set an earlier deadline to allow for slippages. At worst, make sure you know when all your deadlines are so that you don't book a weekend away just when a huge pile of work is expected.

> **Time management is vital if you are going to squeeze everything in.'**
>
> *RACHEL, UNIVERSITY OF THE WEST OF ENGLAND*

Hard work. Thirdly, we can learn from the ant that hard work is not a bad thing. The ant does not lie around asleep not bothering to do what needs to be done. Rather, it zips to and fro gathering food and getting ready for the days ahead. University should not be seen as the path of least effort. You should attend all your lectures and tutorials as well as handing in your work on time. This approach not only reduces the summer stress for revision to make up for lost marks, it also is a powerful witness to your friends that even your university studies are done *'with all your heart, as working for the Lord, not for men'* (Colossians 3:23). Even if it is your least favourite subject, by attending the lectures and working as hard as you can you are showing your friends that Jesus really is your Lord.

So what practical steps can we take? If you are a student then the simplest step is to buy and use a diary or wall planner. If you've got a bit more cash then you might afford a Personal Digital Assistant. A PDA is more like your mum because it reminds you even when you think you've switched it off! Note down your classes and deadlines so you can plan ahead and look for clashes and minimise pressure points. Remember, no one else will do this for you.

Another important thing is to get into a routine. Now I know routines can be taken to an extreme. I heard of one student who optimised the route of every single journey and daily event to save time and effort! I think that kind of routine would drive me mad. Yet it is a good idea to set days of the week when you will stay in and work. At least then you can let your friends know so they don't interrupt you with tempting offers of coffee and chats. You can then make sure you are able to attend your church/Christian Union Bible Study and prayer meeting. You should do all you can to attend Bible Studies. Jesus taught us very clearly in Matthew 6:21 *'where your treasure is, there your heart will be also'*. If you really do love God then you will love his word and want to be at the Bible studies. Whilst certain weeks may not be possible, good planning should allow you to make attendance the norm. The argument that you will be too busy to attend Bible studies is rather weak. Very few of us find it hard to do the things we really want to do! A pattern of non-attendance is likely to leave you spiritually malnourished.

> **'There is always more you could do but you have to remember you are at university to study.'**
>
> *LYDIA, UNIVERSITY OF SHEFFIELD*

A word to parents

And parents, what can you do to help your children prepare for their own time management? Firstly, you can help by not organizing every detail of your teenager's life! Make sure that by the time they are going to university, they are used to planning their time. You will need to give them opportunities to practise organizing themselves so they can learn from their mistakes. Surely a key idea of parenting is to 'let go' gradually of the practical tasks by giving more responsibility to your children.

Secondly (and particularly if you have a son), prepare them for the minor details of survival! Whilst I am proud of the three meals I can cook, I owe more to being in catered accommodation for my survival during university. If you are able to, teach them how to cook and do the laundry before they go—it might even save you weekend loads of ironing when they come home!

And thirdly, and certainly the most challenging, we should set our children an example by managing our own time well. Are we always late, rushing at the last minute—never prepared for the event? Do our children see us panicking for deadlines and making excuses for never attending the mid-week Bible Study? If they do, then we can hardly expect them to manage their time well. We need to set them positive behaviour patterns to follow.

It is often said that our fast-moving western cultures leave us all 'time poor'. On the surface this is certainly true. Yet, often the root cause of this reality is our failure to get our priorities right. We then feel stressed as we try to squeeze in the real priorities around the rather selfish ambitions or lazy patterns of life. I sadly find this too often my experience and am challenged by the example God gives me with the ant. At university, as with future adult life, it always pays to set out our priorities according to biblical principles.

Looking after the pennies
Avoid getting a huge debt

An obvious area that needs suitable planning is money. This is particularly relevant in the current climate in the UK as top-up fees and student debt look set to be here to stay. Over-spending on a tight budget can be all too easy. Part-time work can help but this needs to be carefully thought through so that it does not cause other problems. So, before some practical application, what are the biblical principles students should apply to this important subject of money?

Although money is far from the main topic in the Bible, it does have quite a lot to say about it! And it can all be summarized with Jesus' punchy conclusion that

'You cannot serve both God and Money' (Luke 16:13). And clearly, the argument Jesus was putting forward was that as we serve God, we need to make sure we don't accidentally start serving money. We will consider three basic principles:

1. Money isn't everything. Perhaps the core principle we need to grasp when it comes to money is its transient value. Whilst we might find it easy to agree with the idea that money has no *lasting* value, it is much harder to agree that it has never had any *real* value. The Bible teaches a radical message—that life is much more than accumulating and then spending money! Jesus teaches you to *'Be on your guard against all kinds of greed: a man's life does not consist in the abundance of his possessions'* (Luke 12:15). Fine, we might say, until we have to live next door to people flaunting a great deal more than we have. But 'having stuff' does not make you happier. In fact, having more can often stress us with the fear of losing it and the worry of deciding what to do with it! If you are a Christian student you can conquer your inner greed to want more. You can pursue God and his ways; the freedom that Jesus has given you from the slavery of sin enables you (by God's continual grace) to see that money isn't everything.

2. Wants are not needs. Now I am not going to get bogged down with deciding what is a 'want' and what is a 'need'. But it is important to realize the difference. When the apostle Paul teaches us that *'godliness with contentment is great gain'* he applies this contentment as being content with *'food and clothing'* (see 1 Timothy 6:6-8). And just in case we need extra persuasion, he reminds us that *'we brought nothing into this world, and we can take nothing out of it'*. If we dare to be honest, an awful lot of the 'stuff' we buy comes under wants and not needs. And when you are away at University, the demand to have will be just the same, but the capacity to supply won't! You don't need to be reading for a degree in economics to see that you will have a supply problem if you don't reduce the demand! Incredible as it may seem,

> **'Living within my means meant I had a financially easier time when I graduated.'**
>
> JONATHAN, MANCHESTER METROPOLITAN UNIVERSITY

designer clothes and the latest DVDs are *not* essential to survival! So as a Christian, you need to learn to practise this difficult art of contentment. If you can manage to discern the difference between your true needs and your optional wants you will both save a lot of money and witness to others where your heart is. Jesus said *'where your treasure is, there will your heart be also'* (Matthew 6:21). Ouch!

3. Money is for sharing. We have already seen the biblical principles that there is more to life than money and that many of the things we claim to need are really just optional extras. Now, as if that were not enough, Jesus goes on to teach us that the money that we do have is also to be shared. Let no one convince you that the Christian message is not radical! Some people agree there is more to life than money but often this is because they know they have no hope of ever getting any! Others happily survive on their needs and not their wants because their frugality is really a secret desire to store up money and feel rich! Few of us are genuinely willing to give back to God (and to share with others he places around us) a share of what God has already given to us. All that we have as Christians has come from God. Whether we live off a gift, a wage or a loan, ultimately it has come from God. And so students are also included in the biblical teaching to give some back. If we don't, we are effectively robbing God of what is rightfully his (see Malachi 3:8).

Even as a student you should see the principle of sharing as one that applies to your student money. Whilst this clearly applies to supporting the Lord's work financially in some way, it also applies to our possessions, our hospitality and our own free time. If you really want to serve God in this way, you won't be legalistically arguing what the minimum amount is to give of this and that. If you are doing this, you have missed the point. It's not the amount you give, it's the way you give. Jesus said that *'whatever you did for the least of these brothers of mine, you did for me.'* (Matthew 25:40). And the apostle Paul reminds us that *'God loves a cheerful giver'* in 2 Corinthians 9:7.

By way of practical application to students, you need to plan out a realistic budget of all your costs: accommodation, food, books, clothes, travel, socializing etc and stick to it! If you just spend money without any limits or thought for future bills, it will not be long before you overstretch your funds. The cost of living will vary from location to location and be more in large cities, but do get an idea of what to expect. The best source of information is likely to be an existing student although the university's student union or accommodation office should be able to send you details of typical costs in that area.

If you get paid lump sums (like a grant cheque, bank loan etc) then you might find it helpful to open a savings account and, in effect, pay yourself back each month so that you have a fixed amount of money to deal with a month at a time. In this way, you may more practically avoid eating into future resources rather than overspending and trying to skimp on everything at the end of each term! And when you do budget for the things you do need to buy, avoid the temptation to get the biggest and best available. As a Christian you should be a careful steward of your money. Do you need to buy all the books on your course book list when there is a library? Do your clothes need to have top designer labels when cheaper brands are still fashionable? Do you need a computer with every whiz-bang attachment when you will spend most of your time just typing on it? You can save money simply by being sensible about what you buy.

Some students may need to get work so think ahead about what work is suitable. The most common work for students is bar work either in the students' union or a local pub. Yet this is inappropriate for a Christian. Not only is the environment likely to encourage your own social life to centre on a bar, but actively serving your friends in their own drunkenness is wrong. If you think you will need work then do some research into other jobs that might be available. Many university administration offices take on students for part-time work as do university libraries and cafes. One of my former students landed herself a job working in

'I got a job as a waitress in a restaurant. But then I got roped into serving in the adjoining bar. I wish I had asked about this at the start.'

LENA, ANGLIA POLYTECHNIC UNIVERSITY

the university library. Not only did she get paid at a good rate, she was able to research her own work and gather materials during the quiet evening shifts! If you have found a church to attend you could also mention your need of work to folk there. At best, you might find someone offering part time work. If not, they will know the local geography and businesses that may have something suitable. And of course, it should go without saying that you need to be ahead of the competition if you want to get the most suitable job with the best hours and wage.

Another practical step is to make a budget for giving. If you argue that tithing is only for when you have graduated, you are not only ignoring the scriptural principle we have already seen, you are beginning a bad habit. In reality there is no 'best time' to start other than now. Graduation will bring with it the cost of work, marriage will bring the cost of running a home (and a spouse!). I need not remind you of the cost of having children. There will always be a superficial reason not to start giving, yet Jesus knows our needs. He promises us that if we *'seek first the kingdom of God'*, which means serving God first with our money, then he will supply all our needs (see Matthew 6:33). Don't underestimate how hard this is! Yet do start now before bad habits begin to form.

But above all, learn to be content. You'll meet some seemingly very rich students who will try to make you look inadequate and in serious need of this or that item. But remember that your heavenly Father supplies all your needs, and that your life is more than the sum of all your belongings. You have Christ and he is the pearl of greatest price. Even at university you can show how much you love and value him by not living for, or loving money, more than you love him.

A word to parents

Whilst a great deal of the application on money management is for students, as parents we can also help our children prepare. Firstly we should sit down with our child before he or she goes to plan out what money is needed. Help them to see the real costs and be clear with them about money you will give and when it will be given. Of course, it should go without saying that we then need to honour that promise, provided our circumstances do not dramatically change.

But also, we ought to give our children practice at managing their own money before they go away. Perhaps you could do something like giving your children their own clothes allowance at an earlier age. They will then learn to make tough decisions about what to buy and how to plan for new seasons and major replacements. It is good preparation for the bigger budget they will manage at university. It might also save you the hassle of shopping with them and trying to choose their clothes!

Also, as with the earlier matters, we need to set a good example with our own money management and giving. Are we extravagant spenders? Are we heavily in debt? Do we give to the Lord and share what we have with others? How hard it will be for us to help our own children if we do not practise what we preach!

Unity in the faith

Living with Christians

At university you will quickly learn that not all who call themselves Christians believe or practise what you do. It is a sad reality that over the last two thousand years of church history there has been (and still is) a bewilderingly large variety of biblical interpretations and behaviour. As a young Christian you will need to be prepared for this. Not only will other Christians question and debate with you, but non-Christians will either assume we are all the same or attack us for our disunity. Dealing with difference within the wider Christian church is not easy, and so you do need to be prepared before you arrive. There are three essential biblical principles that we will look at to help us cope with this issue.

1. The Bible is our basis. Our starting point must always be that the Bible is God's inspired and faultless Word such that it is our main and final source of truth. The Puritan Christians had a Latin phrase 'Sola Scriptura' which means Scripture Alone. This sums up that principle. The apostle Paul teaches us in 2 Timothy 3:16 that *'All scripture is God-breathed and is useful for teaching, rebuking, correcting and training in righteousness, so that the man of God may be thoroughly equipped for every good work'*. If our starting point and ending points are Scripture then we have the best hope that we will reach the truth and thus come to unity. Yes, there are textual issues and difficulties with some passages. Yet almost all biblical scholars who have the highest regard and submission to Scripture agree over a great deal of biblical text. No, reading the Bible will not automatically sweep away all the differences but it is and must be the starting point if agreement is ever to be made. The way we are to deal with the difficult passages is to use the clearer ones as lights to shine their truths onto these more difficult ones. We know that the Bible cannot contradict itself because it is written by a God who cannot lie (see Titus 1:2).

> **'In the CU there are people from all over the world meeting together to learn God's word and work on evangelism.'**
>
> SAM, UNIVERSITY OF THE WEST OF ENGLAND

When Jesus taught his disciples he often used Old Testament scriptures to drive home his point. He knew that all that had been written was in agreement with what he was saying. An example of this is his so-called Sermon on the Mount recorded in Matthew 5-7, especially 5:1-48. When the apostle Paul was defending the gospel against Jewish opposition he always used the Old Testament scriptures (see Acts 13:16-44 and Acts 17:2). Paul's authority and basis for his teaching was God's Word. This model of teaching and reasoning is the one we should follow. As a student attempting to debate and talk with other Christians, you should derive and defend your beliefs from the Bible. If you cannot do this and they can then they might be right!

2. Speak in love. When Paul taught the Ephesians why they had been given elders one of the reasons he gives is so they

> **'I very much regret the times I simply argued about other people's lifestyle.'**
>
> *KEVIN, BRADFORD UNIVERSITY*

will be equipped to *'speak the truth in love'* (Ephesians 4:15). Sadly our first principle of 'Sola Scriptura' is often taken without this equally important one of love. In teaching the Corinthians, Paul famously said that if we do not have love we are like *'a resounding gong or a clanging cymbal'* (1 Corinthians 13:1). We need to constantly remind ourselves that whatever light we have from the Scriptures we have by God's grace which has come to us from the Holy Spirit (1 Corinthians 2:14-16). Most evangelicals rightly stand firm on the centrality of Scripture. However they do also seem to have a reputation for arguing their case without much love and care. Yet to win the argument in an unloving way is dishonouring to the Lord. If we claim to live by the Spirit then we should display his fruit. We will have (amongst other qualities) patience and self control (see Galatians 5:25). And yet the greatest of these is love. Someone once said that we can often be quick to teach the importance of the doctrines of grace yet too slow to show the grace that should come from knowing these doctrines. As you engage in lively and spirited debate with other Christians at university, always do so with love.

3. Leave room for conscience. God has wisely given Christians a certain amount of freedom of individual conscience. This should not be stretched to allow personal interpretation to rule the day, but neither should it be squashed so that it cannot be applied to the minor matters where cultural differences are likely. In 1 Corinthians 10:23-33, the apostle Paul outlined this principle in the context of eating meat offered to idols. Paul's argument was that whilst meat is just meat and idols are powerless, nevertheless we should respect another person's conscience if *he* is worried about eating such meat. Although there may be no absolute wrong we should seek the good of the other person and not violate his conscience. Now of course this isn't easy in practice because the argument continues over what is a 'conscience matter'! One person's matter of conscience may be another person's down-the-line essential biblical teaching. On some matters of detail it may be better to leave a difference for the sake of unity and fellowship rather than squeeze every last drop of conformity. How can we decide this? Well, remember again that James teaches us that *'if any of you lacks wisdom, he should ask God'* (James 1:5).

By way of application then to students, the aim in speaking with your brother or sister should be their growth in grace. If they are new believers, do not burden them with issues that they cannot yet be expected to understand. Some people will have entirely different church backgrounds and you should exercise patience to judge when (if ever) it is appropriate for you to start or to continue a debate on a particular issue. It is all too easy just to aim at winning an argument or even (sadly) to show superior biblical knowledge rather than to aim to build the other person up. As an undergraduate from a very conservative background, I sadly enjoyed quoting from this and that passage more than listening to the real needs of my friends.

You should also avoid discussions that, as Jesus put it, *'strain out a gnat but swallow a camel.'* (Matthew 23:24). Too much attention can easily be spent on minor issues when there are either major issues that do need to be debated or that are already agreed on! Whilst as individual Christians you may end up attending a different church (quite rightly) because of differences, these differences may not need to divide and thus spoil your fellowship at other times. I have met Christians who seem only to be happy when they have found something to disagree on! Where then is the opportunity to *'encourage one another and build each other up'*? (1 Thessalonians 5:11).

However, having made the point for encouraging agreement and fellowship *where appropriate* you do also need to watch out for serious error that might do you real harm. The apostle Peter warns us about such 'false teachers' that can lead us to ruin (See 2 Peter 2:1-22). Universities are sometimes breeding grounds for cults and single-issue sects, and so you need to be able to discern between false and true teachers. Even spending lots of social time with such people can be dangerous. When I was an undergraduate, a group teaching that baptism was essential for salvation caused a great deal of trouble and even led to a ban on all religious groups in the student hall where I lived. Whilst no single test is likely to discern all issues, a good starting question to 'see where a person is' might be to ask what he or she is depending on to get to heaven. If the person doesn't clearly point to the finished work of Christ alone given to them entirely by God's grace, then you will have fundamental differences and need to tread carefully.

Another helpful guide someone gave to me was the four major aspects of true Christianity:
1. accepting the sufficiency and authority of scripture,
2. believing the centrality and vitality of the Cross,
3. having an ongoing personal relationship with God, and
4. submitting to the Lordship of Christ.

If you can make friends with other students who believe these fundamental truths, they are likely to do you good and you will have good fellowship. Students who do not hold these views may well be Christians (albeit poorly taught). The Lord doesn't want you to bash them to pieces by exposing their mistakes; rather, he wants you to demonstrate God's grace in you by building them up in their faith (Romans 15:1-6).

But perhaps the most important preparation you need is practical experience in the art of handling the scriptures. Whilst you won't have all the answers at your fingertips, you can help cope with your many student discussions by going to university with a good grounding in *how to study the Bible*. You need to know the fundamentals of the faith and I recommend http://www.christianbasics.org/ as one such study course to follow. You could use this as a guide to teaching others whom you meet. As well as knowing the fundamentals in your head, you need to know how to reason them from the Scriptures. If you cannot do this for the easier subjects, you will have no hope with the trickier 'hot topics'. Study God's Word now so that it is not an unfamiliar book to you when someone asks you a question. How would you go about teaching someone about God's sovereignty? Where would you turn to show that Jesus is the exclusive way to God?

Finally, do not regard difference as something to be avoided at all costs. Whilst you must agree with others on the fundamentals of the faith to have any meaningful fellowship, Christian debate can and should be a good thing. Not only will it strengthen your understanding of what you do believe and sift out your misunderstandings, it will also encourage you as you see that the Bible *does* stand up to close scrutiny. You should have no no-go areas; by debating with others you will see that God's truth is both consistent and credible!

A word to parents

Whilst the main application has again been to students, as parents we can play two important roles in helping our children prepare for the debates and discussions with other Christians.

It again goes without saying that we must teach our children the fundamentals of the faith. But we should do more than that. We should encourage them in the art of systematic Bible study themselves by taking them to our local church weekly Bible studies. And to do this we must be in regular attendance too not only to demonstrate its importance but also for the very practical matter of getting our child there and back! Attending the church Bible study not only shows our child how our elders (and other Christians) handle the scriptures, but it will also expose them to a wider range of biblical issues in proportion to their appearance in the Bible. For example, the doctrines of grace show up in just about every chapter of every book. Yet the matter of what style of singing we ought to have in church doesn't! As parents we are often very good at showing our children how important school work is and how they ought to put this ahead of sport and relaxation. Yet we can easily make the mistake of putting academic preparation and study ahead of the spiritual. If we do, we are robbing our children of important teaching they will need at university and important practise in properly handling the scriptures. If our children watch (and also participate) in group Bible study in their home church, they will be better prepared for this at university. They may well be the only person in their hall who is willing or able to lead Bible studies that will teach other young believers.

The second area we can help our children with is in instilling a gracious and balanced spirit when it comes to lesser matters. In writing this I certainly do not suggest that these matters are unimportant such that 'any view is acceptable'. However, some matters are clearly *less important* than others. We should teach our children to focus on the greater matters not only because they are greater but because understanding (and thus agreement) on lesser matters will almost never come if there is no understanding or agreement on the greater. The light and understanding from the greater makes teaching the lesser much easier. Therefore, whilst we should teach our children matters of worship order, church government and particular social habits, we should not major on them to the extent that they dominate our homes. More significantly, any teaching we do give *must* be clearly derived from the greater matters so that our children can teach rather than merely parrot talk our teaching. Why is this particularly important at university? Well, because external differences are far more obvious than other differences and therefore have a natural tendency to dominate debates. If your children have been home-schooled this will become immediately apparent to other Christians. Yet is that the topic that should be debated most of the time? If we practise a gracious and balanced spirit in dealing with these lesser issues, we serve our children well to copy us and do the same. Starting debates at the 'wrong end' quickly leads to legalism. In Paul's letter to the Romans he spends eleven chapters reworking the gospel before explaining their rightful responses. It is only in Romans 12:1 that we read *'Therefore, I urge you brothers, in view of God's mercy, to offer your bodies as living sacrifices....'* We can help our children by showing them how to major on God's mercy before moving to lesser issues that only honour God when they come from such motivation.

> 'It is essential to rise above secondary issues.'
>
> *DANIEL, EDGE HILL UNIVERSITY, ORMSKIRK*

To an unknown God

Witnessing to your friends

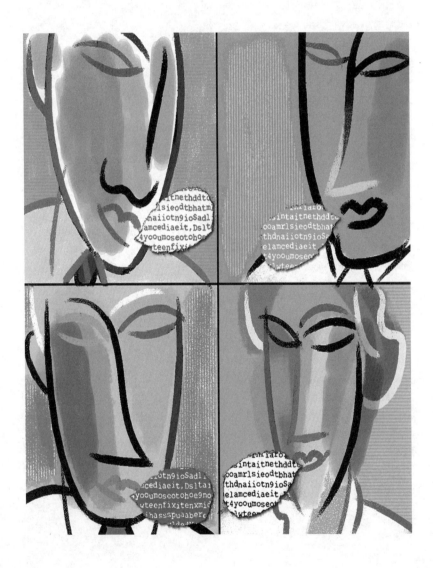

Whilst some people who have never been to university criticize them as being unreal, isolated enclaves they fail to notice one dominant reality: universities are full of unbelievers and thus share a great deal of the realities of the wider world. Whilst universities are 'unreal' in some ways (where else do people have five months off from a full-time occupation?) they are certainly real in terms of their domination by unbelievers. Yet university, having unbelievers with huge amounts of time to think and question the big issues of life, is an *ideal* place both for formal mission and informal personal evangelism.

Almost every university will have a Christian Union (a CU), which is a body of students who have a certain pot of money from the university's funds to run a 'club or society for students to join'. The CU should not become a substitute for a church quite simply because it isn't one. It will not be structured or governed according to biblical principles nor is it likely to have suitable leaders to undertake full biblical teaching and pastoring. Neither of these is a problem as the CU is not intended to be the university's church. Rather, it is a union for the purpose of informal fellowship amongst Christians and a focus for student led mission and evangelism. And provided that the CU is evangelical and sticks to its purpose of promoting Christ to students, it is worth joining. Most CUs operate on a democratic basis because they are required to by university rules. Therefore, even if you think some of the leadership are skewed in their theology, you can have a good influence if you are wise and mature in informing the agenda and direction whilst you are there. Mission and evangelism are huge subjects so I have chosen to divide this into three sections that consider biblical principles that apply to three very different audiences and then to apply each in turn. I suggest you are likely to have opportunities to witness to three fundamentally different types of unbeliever:

> **'Unlike the Church, the CU has no biblical authority structure to govern and ensure restraint.'**
>
> *JAMES, UNIVERSITY OF WALES, ABERYSTWYTH*

1. neutral unbelievers who just want to find out what it is all about,

2. religious unbelievers who hold other views yet want to debate the differences with Christianity, and
3. ambivalent unbelievers who don't really believe anything (so they say) yet who do have big questions about life.

There are probably better ways of classifying people but I suggest everyone is covered by one of these three. I have not included those students who are openly hostile to the Christian faith and who refuse to listen as Jesus taught his disciples not to waste time on such people (see Matthew 10:14). How do you reach these people above—what approaches can you take? Whilst there are a good many more, these ideas are a start.

1. Neutral unbelievers. In many ways students we meet who are peaceful and open to hear our message are the easiest for us to cope with. This means we can probably make the quickest progress in getting to the heart of evangelism: teaching directly from the Scriptures. The apostle Paul clearly teaches that someone can be saved ultimately only by hearing the word of God (Romans 10:12-15). This is an important point because some other Christians you meet will suggest that we should used modern alternatives to get our message across. Their argument goes that just as books are old fashioned but films all the rage, so the Bible is less useful than film and drama. This is undoubtedly true for many things, yet we are to follow God's ways and not our own! Watching a film about Jesus may not be wrong but it should never replace God's Word. So if you have the opportunity to use it, then don't miss your chance. Your words spoken from the Bible might well be the method God uses to bring his salvation to them.

In application for preparation, you could advertise a series of short talks for a bigger group as a CU event or short Bible studies for one or two people as a private event in hall. The study given at http://www.christianbasics.org/could be a starting template. The important thing with this approach is to go only as fast as the hearers are able to go. Pray before each event that God will use the teaching and resulting discussion to reveal his truth. Carefully but firmly keep the discussion on the main subject at hand. It is all too easy to get side tracked down blind alleys that generate a great deal of heat but little light.

2. Religious unbelievers. Perhaps the greatest surprise you will have is when you talk to people who follow other religions. They may follow a religion you know a little about like Islam or Judaism. Or they may follow a less well known religion like Hinduism, Sikhism, or Zoroastrianism. You are also likely to meet people who are Jehovah's Witnesses, Seventh Day Adventists, Mormons or Quakers. How on earth do you witness to any of these?

Well we can learn again from the example Jesus gave us when he spoke to the Jewish believers in his day. When Jesus spoke to the Pharisees he always referred to what they *believed* and then compared this to the true Old Testament scriptures (see Matthew 15:1-20). It is true to say Jesus did at times condemn the Pharisee's actions (like the money changing in the temple in Matthew 21:12-14). However, his main approach was to deal with their teaching and to compare this to his truth.

This is the approach we are better taking when witnessing to people from other religions. If we try to attack the wrong done by people who follow their religion (like wars, persecution and violence) this not only causes unhelpful offence, but leads the discussion away from the gospel. Also, it can leave us exposed to counter-claims of wrong done in the name of Christianity. Rather than attack or debate behaviour, we ought to focus on their teaching. Where does their holy book come from? Does God claim to be its author and does it stand up to cross-checking? What does it say about God? How does it explain sin and trouble in the world? What is its answer and is it either reliable or possible? None of these questions will guarantee easy answers, but they will help you to focus the discussion on the important issues. God's Word is reliable and certain, and it is unique in teaching that it is God himself who provides salvation and that his salvation is complete and guaranteed to work!

Witnessing to believers from other religions needs to be done with care and respect. Where you can, accommodate their cultural and legitimate preferences. Paul said that he became like Jews to win Jews and like others to win them (see 1 Corinthians 9:19-23).

Do some research on the main teachings of these other religions so that you can show an interest. Be willing to find out what they do believe and ask careful but direct questions where the teaching falls short of the truth. If you engage your friends on matters of truth, you not only avoid offence, but you increase the opportunity to speak of Christ.

Ambivalent unbelievers. Perhaps the biggest grouping of students you will have opportunities to reach are those who just wander through life not really thinking about religion. They have probably discounted it as old-fashioned or boring, yet they still have many big unanswered questions.

When the apostle Paul was in Athens waiting for his fellow workers to arrive, he saw a city full of people claiming to be wise yet acting foolishly. The Athenians loved thinking and debating how to live, but at the same time were steeped in idolatry. Their idols were not conceptual like those people worship today; they were physical lumps of wood or stone! And so faced with this situation of ambivalent unbelievers who didn't know the first thing

> **'Students are generally more open to talk about different world views.'**
>
> *GERARD, DE MONTFORD UNIVERSITY*

about the true God or the Bible, Paul shows wise flexibility in changing his model for preaching. Instead of speaking directly from the Scriptures, he assessed the best theme to follow and then presented an *entirely scriptural* argument but using their own language and culture. You can read the whole account in Acts 17:16-34. He saw an inscription to 'an unknown god' and used this as a starting point to introduce the God who created them and to show that if God is great, then how can he be squashed into a lump of stone? If we are like God then how foolish it was to think that a stone was like us! And once he had caught their attention and opened the holes in their argument, he skilfully presents Christ and his resurrection to show how the real God has demonstrated his power and his authority to judge them.

Practical suggestions

So, in application, you can legitimately follow Paul's approach when your audience or individual friend clearly has no knowledge of the Bible or any real interest in seeking God. Whilst the topic of 'Origins' is a popular and sometimes-helpful starting point, it can also lead into blind alleys if you don't well research your material. Others topics you could use are:

1. Is there justice in this world?
2. Why is there no peace and security?
3. What is causing the collapse of society?

This list is clearly not exhaustive, but it does have three topics that many people ask about. From each of these you can show God's answer and how Jesus is central to all three. Remember that Paul was not interested in winning an argument—he was interested in preaching Christ. If your audience doesn't know the Bible, don't use it. Start where they are and pray that you have a second opportunity to follow up more specific teaching from the Bible at a later date.

At university you will have many wonderful opportunities to witness and speak about Christ. Make it your aim to use these opportunities wisely. Go prepared with different strategies for different people. Get involved in your CU and influence it for good. You may want to promote and develop these ideas to produce materials and activities that target these people. The apostle Paul was wise, flexible and, above all, always focussed on preaching Christ. Sometimes he could speak directly, other times indirectly. You have a wonderful opportunity to bring many more into God's marvellous light!

Renewing your mind
Change the World!

When I started my MSc, I was taken (along with everyone else on my course) into a lecture theatre for an introductory lecture. The dean bounced in with a beaming smile and assured us that our future was bright. We were the best engineers in the world (his reasoning was that we had not yet made any mistakes) and an exciting future was before us. Whilst at times I did feel like I had taken a wrong turn into an army boot camp, his inspiring ideas and encouragement to think big were very helpful.

Youth is a time for dreaming. Amongst all the day-to-day activities at university, don't lose time to sit back and question what you are learning and what is going on in the world. You need to think about why you do things and the content of your course. Your university subjects (at least some) are meant to provoke you to ask questions and to challenge the status quo.

Universities have historically been the birthplace of radical, even revolutionary ideas. Political and social change has often developed from student debates, which have fired up generations to bring great change. Some of these revolutions have been based on ideals of justice and freedom. In the West, much recent change has come from more selfish desires to promote ungodly ideas of moral freedom and the right to do wrong. But why should it stay like this? As a Christian you not only have a radical message to tell, but a powerful God to help you. The apostle Paul saw the need for this type of radical thinking when he said *'do not conform any longer to the pattern of this world, but be transformed by the renewing of your mind'* (Romans 12:2).

Being an engineer, many would say I come from the rather tame corner of the world for possible revolutions. When we engineers are not buried in the detailed optimisation of a particular product, our horizons rarely move further than dreaming of innovative technologies to make even bigger or faster products! But even engineers who are Christians can dream of ways to significantly develop other parts of the world to improve living standards or to design products that promote better stewardship of God's resources! Whatever you are studying, ask big questions about why things are as they are. Is your subject heavily based on humanist thinking? Then how can you change this? Science, history, geography, and anthropology—the list is almost endless. What about the social issues that dominate our lives? Ethics, feminism, sexuality, poverty, debt, consumerism, war?

Jesus teaches us that we Christians *are* the salt of the earth. We are the *only* true light of the world (Matthew 5:13-16). Perhaps like no other time of your life, at university you will have both the time and the environment to engage in truly radical Christian thinking. Consider of all the ways as a Christian that you would like to change yourself and the world. Use your time well. Get a grip on the Bible and study it book by book. Aim to read it all and set time aside to pray over what you read. You could start informal research groups to share ideas and gather new material to inform your thinking. You could set up debates with other students to promote a wider discussion.

University can and should be a great experience. Don't see your time there as just a means to an end. Make it your goal at university to please God. I don't expect people like Lord Shaftesbury, William Wilberforce or Elizabeth Fry in their younger years imagined they would inspire great change. Yet by renewing their minds and calling upon God they did. Why not set your mind on doing the same?

Appendix
Internet Links

Whilst I cannot personally endorse all they contain, the following Internet sites do provide a great deal of useful information.

University/Church Information
University Application Information
http://www.ucas.ac.uk/
Information on UK Universities
http://www.hero.ac.uk/
University & Colleges Christian Fellowship
http://www.uccf.org.uk/
Grace Baptist Church Directory
http://www.grace.org.uk/
FIEC Church Directory
http://www.fiec.co.uk/
Find a Church Directory
http://www.findachurch.co.uk/
Evangelical Churches in Wales
http://www.aecw.org.uk/churchesix.htm

Personal Management
Credit Action
http://www.creditaction.org.uk/
Charities Aid Foundation
http://www.cafonline.org/uk_default.cfm
Support for Learning
http://www.support4learning.org.uk/money/
Successful Study Skills

http://bubl.ac.uk/link/s/studyskills.htm
Spiritual Preparation
http://users.aber.ac.uk/emk/ap/univ.htm

Bible Study/Christian Ethics
Christian Basics
http://www.christianbasics.org/
Free Bible Software
http://www.e-sword.net/
The Christian Institute
http://www.christian.org.uk/
The Evangelical Library
http://www.elib.org.uk/index.html
The On-line Bible
http://www.onlinebible.org/
Christian Classics: Ethereal Library
http://www.ccel.org
Puritan and Reformed writings
http://puritansermons.com/index.htm
Bible Gateway
http://www.biblegateway.com/
Online Christian Bookshop
http://www.tabernaclebookshop.org
The Cambridge Papers
http://www.jubilee-centre.org/cambridge_papers/index.php
English L'Abri
http://www.englishlabri.org/
Christian Counterculture Project
http://www.christiancounterculture.org/

Evangelism
Answers in Genesis
http://www.answersingenesis.org/
Reformed Apologetics & Theology

http://www.reformed.org/

Free Grace Tracts

http://www.free-grace.org.uk/Library/bookindex.htm

World Religions Information

http://bubl.ac.uk/link/linkbrowse.cfm?menuid=2595

Who is Jesus?

http://www.whoisjesus-really.com/english/default.htm

Personal Evangelism

http://rsglh.org/personal.evangelism.how.htm

© Day One Publications 2005   First printed 2005

All Scripture quotations are taken from the New International Version

A CIP record is held at The British Library   ISBN 1 903087 82 1

Published by Day One Publications Ryelands Road, Leominster, HR6 8NZ

☎ 01568 613 740 FAX 01568 611 473   email—sales@dayone.co.uk www.dayone.co.uk

Editor: Jim Holmes

Design and Art Direction: Steve Devane Illustrations: Susan LeVan   Printed by Gutenberg Press, Malta